Behind the Shade

Behind the Shade

Lionel Bannerman

ISBN: Softcover   978-1-5434-9290-3
             eBook   978-1-5434-9289-7

Rev. date: 10/09/2018

To order additional copies of this book, contact:
Xlibris
800-056-3182
www.Xlibrispublishing.co.uk
Orders@Xlibrispublishing.co.uk
786171

CONTENTS

ACKNOWLEDGEMENT

It has been a journey full of 'ups' and 'downs' but at the end, this book has become a reality.

I would like to thank the many people who have helped with this book. My deepest gratitude goes to Evangelist Mark Cofie Awudey. When Brother Mark says meet me at 8:00am, you would meet him at the venue minutes before time and is a Man of his Word. Wesley Methodist Sunday School (Sekondi-Ghana), Kingdom Light Outreach (K.L.O), First Love Church – film stars (Lighthouse Chapel) especially Rebecca [title reserved] and to my fellow colleagues at the Ghana Technology University College (GTUC).

My dad (William 'Jones' Clegg): Who has imbibed the habit of reading to his children (Leolin, Ivan, Thyra). An honourable father who never gives up in his dreams, obeys time and just.

My mum (Rebecca Clegg): For providing me with a booklet to compile all written articles and persistency in developing the stories.

My siblings: For their support and love.

It has also been an honour to have met Benjamin Nortey (Paa Nii), Ebo Awortwe, Adwoa Awukubea Asare, Albert Yankey and Lyanne Sackey for reminding me constantly not to give up on the book.

For all who encouraged the birth of this book by motivating and giving their individual suggestions, I say thank you.

God Bless You All.

PREFACE

This book was written mainly on observations in life. Many of the things that occur around us could either be something to learn from or be taken for granted. In the prison cell, the longing to see the trees, feel the effect of the wind on the body, the sight of the birds is a gem which cannot be gotten. Soldiers after coming back from the war zone, look forward to meeting their families and having time with them. There is much hope the writer observed especially when a visit to the hospital tells of the state of man which could change by events. Individuals complain about circumstances that may not be favourable, point fingers at persons but deep inside us, how does one develop his or her self. The things we read, watch and hear shapes our mentality to think in particular ways. The association Man involves himself in, leads him to be positive or negative in the way of life. Gifts and opportunities are not visible to the human eye but a prepared person sees it when the chance presents itself. Our true self should not be a photocopy of someone. Being you and working to being a better person is dependent on us. Changing the wrong habits is a step to being a better person, doing the same thing every day will produce the same result. The writer seeks to enlighten all about things in our environment which is copied blindly because everyone seems to be following a particular trend.

The trees which shed forth their leaves in their season, the hustle and bustle of the early morning traffic, the lives of individuals over a period of time and what their end became are a part of some things the writer took notice of.

Listen! Wisdom is calling out. Reason is making herself heard.
On the hilltops near the road and at the crossroads she stands.
At the entrance to the city, beside the gates, she calls:
"I appeal to all of you; I call to everyone on earth...
Proverbs 8

CHAPTER ONE

The Early Stages of Learning and Growth

MY BIRTH

I wish I was born in a foreign land. Britain probably, so I can complain about the land which is not sufficient for farming or the lack of minerals in the soil to export so that my country would be rich. I prefer a country with enough water such as Japan, so I can visit the beach and enjoy the weather. The atomic bomb being released years ago has kept me silent, the land is also not enticing, I am sure all nations know but it is my excuse for not doing well so I need support from neighbouring countries. Let me try a different country now, Germany, this country was partitioned into two; east and west. Now it is one but beer is what is common, the water from the land is not as nice as other countries. Water is the main substance the human body needs, so I cannot function fully since my basic need has been altered.

I am in relations with my Maker as to where he would want to place me. I find myself in a continent and country too. We need one another to function, to motivate ourselves and do bigger things. This nation is alone, not much mineral resources, there is land and water around it but "two heads are better than one". All countries are together at least, I need to board a plane to get to the country of my choice whether close or far.

Living in an island like the Pacific Ocean would be fun. I would see the penguins, bears and stay in the igloos. There is petroleum, diamond, gold, uranium, tin and so on. Oh, I can stay here, it's perfect for me. The plants and animals can make life wonderful. My worry is I have no fashion agency here. I need a place to get clothes, it's too cold. I am rich here but I have to keep warm by wearing the heavy boots with designer labels inscribed on.

Can I get a place so rich and warm, not isolated so that I wouldn't have to argue with my Maker as to where he wants me to be.

I am in a country in Africa where all things are similar and countries seem to have so many resources. The weather is not in a constant cold or hot condition, it balances itself when necessary. The soil is good to produce natural food and hosts some wild animals and rare species. It's a wonderful sight to marvel at. It has everything I could ever dream of. I have lived in here and seem to be comfortable but I have realized one thing amongst the people in the land. We don't love ourselves much; we trade what we have for what we want. We give our resources away, corruption has eaten the good of the land. If all the countries in this continent were one, it would have been none to be compared to. The difference between the rich and poor is so glaring that it is disheartening to know. Natural disasters are not frequent here but as a country under the umbrella of this continent, I complain of lack of money from my own land. I take funds from the countries and continents who wished were me but are not.

My siblings are spread out like roots in all continents, yet do very well. What more do I wish to have to be a better person. What lessons am I not learning from my siblings who make it despite me not being born there. Is it due to the colour of my skin, my upbringing or something in me I haven't identified? I have all it takes to make myself comfortable, produce food, clothes, manufacture anything and everything, build anything I could ever dream of. Yet, I am so dependent on my siblings, without them I don't know where and how I would be. They clothe, feed and take what I have because I have not seen the use of what I have till I have lost it all probably.

THE LEARNING PHASE

At 8pm, the event of the day begins to play to Obed once more. When he brushes his teeth, he soils himself with the paste as it first circles his mouth and drops into his shirt like the splatter of raindrops. He misses the tooth paste on the brush after the first few tries. He is being yelled at by mum who tells him to do it right. The next successive tries was fruitful as he scrapes the wall of the tooth with the brush meticulously. The new uniform and bag with food flask in his hand, was a beauty to behold. Obed baths in a bowl of water, outside the very house he sleeps in but in a compound which shared three other houses with the bathrooms separated from them. He fills the pail with water to wash off the foam on his body in haste for a lovely breakfast. He stepped off the big bowl with his bare feet as he smells 'Tom Brown' emanating from the kitchen. It is a wonderful cereal enjoyed by his dad too.

Obed goes to school for the first day of re-opening and he is amazed to see kids of his kind there. Those who were of the same height as his were there, the girls in a long dress of the same uniform, the cries from the room and the helter-skelter by some other kids across the corridor. Some other kids were calm and reserved, others trying to bully the feeble ones and the amazing experience of going to the assembly in a 'military parade' and learning the national anthem for the first time. It sounded nice as he placed his hand on the left breast, looking up and mimicking the words for the first time.

Class time begins and a tall figure walks in the room with a decorated bag on her left arm and a cane on the right. Obed asked himself what this bag was made of, that had the colours intelligently blended to form a nice piece like that of the spider's web he destroyed back at home. As Obed thought aloud, a gentleman of a shorter height greets her and says "I like your kente bag". Her lips spread across from both ends in a stretching manner which lasted for a while.

The clinging of the bell in the noon had everyone rushing out for the closing session of the day. Most of the students begun waling home and the chattering was low among themselves. Alex was a kid from my neighbourhood who joined me to dad's car that afternoon. We ride home in the moving vehicle as a song is played on the radio. Obed asks dad what the song means and he says it is called 'Yenara Asaase ni', a national anthem in the local language. The song talks about the land Ghana which has been given to us, the citizens, to cherish and uphold. In good and bad, it would depend on us to decide.

The alarm chimes and Obed wakes up realising it's been a dream and a long night, as he prepares to take on the challenges for the new day. This dream occurs due to a visit to school with his dad the day before.

A DREAM

Kofi is a seven-year-old boy who walks for hours barefoot to the next village for school. He wakes up at 4am to fetch water for the house with a sick dad and an aunt who helps run the home by cooking and administering drugs with the right prescription from the only pharmaceutical shop, found in the village of about 5km from home. The Pharmacist happens to be the only National Service person, assisting in the health welfare of the village and its environs. He is a dedicated young chap who serves whole heartedly and loved by all.

By 6 am, Kofi would fetch mushrooms in a sack to get some money for fees and the health care of the household. He is dressed in his 'Kokonte and abenkwan' uniform (which is to say the yellow shirt and brown shorts or skirts for girls being worn from primary to the junior high school in the government schools in Ghana) which is pressed neatly. The box iron with hot charcoals from the pot is the magic behind the glowing uniform. These charcoals would be poured out when everyone is done ironing for the day. He would go to school late and not concentrate fully at school due to tiredness from the farm. His mum who had died from an ailment was one thing that would not depart from his mind, for she was loving and one who lifts the spirits of all by that beautiful widespread smile of hers and humour.

Kofi's mum used to go to the stream, fetch water in the calabash with a baby at the back wrapped and pregnant in front. This, the mum did virtually throughout her stay in the mud house among the compound houses which surrounded them. It has been two years since the mum's departure and in spite of these challenges; he knew he would love to be the General Secretary of the United Nations with Kofi Annan as his mentor. He would stay back after school with a teacher who loved him dearly, staying till 6:30pm, for some clarity of topics and into some other subjects which is scheduled throughout the week. This he did sacrificially since he discovered his potential of becoming a brilliant student. Kofi's ability to understand quickly and apply the knowledge acquired to suit his environment especially in the science and arts subjects, was one of the many signs seen by the teacher.

Kofi grew into an adult faster with the passage of time as he took care of his responsibilities at home very well. He learnt how to trade, invest, buy foodstuffs from the market and talk to the elderly with ease. He used to be shy in his childhood days but had to adapt to being self confident and read lots of books. He became the Head of the Debators' Club at school which boosted his confidence, making him believe he was climbing the ladder a step at a time to achieve his purpose as the General Secretary one day. It is step by step, he muffled to himself. There is a lake which divides his village from the market in the neighbouring village. This young man would cross whenever he had gathered enough mushrooms to sell in the morning. There were accidents once a while from stumps of trees in the water which damaged weaker vessels crossing the lake.

He sold lots of items and rendered services to the community which made him feel proud of himself as a young man, able to provide not only for himself but for his family. Two years ago, as he crossed the lake to the other side, a tree stump pierced his boat. He had not learnt how to swim and he struggled to lean onto a floating board. How he managed to survive was a miracle which led to his right arm being broken. He was insulted by the elderly when taking money or greeting because he used his left hand. They had not figured out his arm was injured. Greeting with the right arm is a norm in the Ghanaian culture which shows a sign of respect. All who bought from the young man admired him and he earned more than the average with skill and enthusiasm. He was humble even when he had more than enough to himself.

A Minister of State met Kofi and his life changed from then. He had the opportunity to climb the highest step of the ladder in his academics in Ghana and became the Secretary- General at age 38. The arm of Kofi was attended to for some years, which became better and unnoticed of a scar in his thought as a 'one-handed-man'. Well, he used the disabled arm to his advantage with the numerous skills acquired.

Constructing a good road, providing social amenities to the villages which lacked them and a hope to kids especially to the disadvantaged ones was a routine each time the gentleman stepped foot in his homeland. He reigned for long and served with fairness in the position of a Secretary- General. He is now old and encourages his grand sons and daughters that it is not by might to be wealthy but it is the Lord who gives. He taught them to be hardworking and be hopeful always. The tune of 'Yenara Asaase' played in his car each time.

THE FIRST BORN

The first born is the beginning or birth of a new life. The first born could be the first child in a couple's life, the first complete project, the first batch of a school and many more. It could also be the shining star in the family of many who have excelled out of the odds by getting to a respectable height in the family.

There is a blessing on the 'first born' in that, he or she is an example for others to follow. The first born is a reference of a feat which has been established by a person or persons. This could be child-bearing, a published book or a dream of a vision which has come to reality.

The 'first-born' is not necessarily the first person born by a parent, though in the right nature it is the blessing of the first child I am referring to. The third born in a family could have the first breakthrough in getting married or starting a business and it could be an open door for the family to progress. This avenue created by this third born is a 'first' in his own way by opening doors and giving hope even to the eldest of the family.

The 'first-born' is the first bold step one takes and finds fulfilment in. It could be a project done for long periods of years which has finally been completed. It could be the first job of many jobs which one can easily remember because of the zeal and passion with which the expectation of what the 'job world' was like. 'First born's' are necessary because it defines the path one treads on for long periods of years usually and gives boldness to try new things. Many things are established when the first of things become a reality. The 'first born' lies in each person which is the ability to innovate, create, solve problems and do things differently from what has been known of as the normal procedure or sequence to achieve a result. The Apostle Paul describes Timothy as his true child in the faith. There are many **firstborns** in this world who have inherited the blessing of other Men through service such as Elisha in the bible.

It is said that there is nothing new under the sun. This does not mean that nothing should be done because it exists. When one accomplishes an achievement by himself or herself, it is a confidence boosting machine that makes an individual proud of doing greater things though it's been done already by other persons.

(But we ought always to give thanks to God for you, brothers beloved by the Lord, because God chooses you as the **first fruits** to be saved, through sanctification by the Spirit and belief in the truth. To this he called you through our gospel, so that you may obtain the glory of our Lord Jesus Christ – 2 Thessalonians 2:13-14). This explains why the first son or daughter in a family is not necessarily a 'FIRST BORN'. We are called by Grace unto Salvation.

Fun Facts on First borns

- Some famous first born children: Albert Einstein, Dan Rather, Oprah Winfrey, Winston Churchill and Colonel Sanders.
- More than half of the United States Presidents were first born children.
- Twenty-one (21) of the twenty-three (23) first astronauts were first born children.
- Two-thirds of entrepreneurs are first born children [1]

A Look into some individuals who made it but were not the first children from their parents

These are some individuals who made it out of the odds to make it in their family without necessarily being the first sons or daughters from their respective parents. Some of these individuals would be described briefly as 'first born's' in their respective accomplishments.

Michael Jordan

Michael Jordan was born in February 17, 1963 in Brooklyn, New York. Growing up in Wilmington, North Carolina, Jordan developed a competitive edge at an early age. His father, James, noted, "What he does have is a competition problem. He was born with that... the person he tries to outdo most of the time is himself." Jordan loved sports but failed to make his high school basketball team as a sophomore. [14] He was told he wasn't good enough, he didn't believe it and went home crying. Michael continued to practice and made the team the next year. After high school he accepted a basketball scholarship to the University of North Carolina, where he played under head coach Dean Smith. [11] When Michael Jordan was in his sophomore (2nd) year, he made an effort for the varsity basketball group but was rejected by the coach which left him devastated but accepted the rejection as a challenge. He strove to enhance his approach and playing style to overcome his lack [13]. Michael based his spirit of dedication to improving on himself as a sports profession.

Michael was signed by the Chicago Bulls which was a losing team. He quickly turned things around and in his first season, he was named to the All-Star team and was later honoured as the league's Rookie of the Year. A broken foot sidelined Jordan for 64 games during the 1985 – 1986 season but he scored 49 points on his return against the Boston Celtics in the first game and 63 in the second game which is an NBA playoff record. [12]

His father, James R. Jordan Snr, was murdered by two teenagers in North Carolina which led to his early retirement of the sports.

Emily Dickinson

She was an American poet born in Amherst, Massachusetts. She lived much of her life in reclusive isolation. Considered an eccentric by locals, she became known for her reluctance to greet guests, even to leave her bedroom. This was as a result from the mid-1850s, Emily's mother became effectively bedridden with various chronic illnesses until her death in 1882. She loved her father that she wrote to a friend in summer 1858. Emily said that she would visit if she could leave "home, or mother. I do not go out at all, lest father will come and miss me, or miss some little act, which I might forget, should I run away". Dickinson's domestic responsibilities weighed more heavily upon her and she confined herself within the Homestead. Emily took this role as her own, and "finding the life with her books and nature so congenial, continued to live it".

Emily lived in a prominent but not wealthy family. She was described by her Aunt Lavinia as perfectly well and contented, a good child with little trouble. Her Aunt also discovered Emily's love for music and her particular talent for the piano which she called "the moosic".

While Emily's father followed up on their education and wrote letters when on business trips, Emily's mother was described as cold and aloof. Daniel Taggart Fiske, the School's Principal (Amherst Academy) at that time recalled that Dickinson was a very bright and an excellent scholar, faithful in all her school duties. Although she had a few terms off due to illness, of which the longest was in 1845 – '46, when she enrolled for only eleven weeks.

Dickinson was troubled from a young age by the "deepening menace" of death, especially the deaths of those who were close to her. Sophia Holland, was one of such persons. She was Emily's second cousin and a close friend, she grew ill from *typhus* and died in April, 1844. This traumatized young Emily. Recalling the incident two years later, Emily wrote that "it seemed to me I should die too if I could not be permitted to watch over her or even look at her face". This made her become so melancholic that her parents sent her to Boston to recover.

Though Dickinson was a prolific poet in private life, fewer of her books were published out of nearly 1,800 pieces written in her lifetime. Withdrawing more and more from the outside world, Emily began in the summer of 1858 what would be her lasting legacy. Reviewing poems she had written previously, she began making clean copies of her work, assembling carefully pieced-together manuscript books. The forty fascicles or bundles she created from 1858 through 1865 eventually held nearly eight hundred poems. No one was aware of the existence of these books until after her death. The published works were altered by publishers to suit the conventional poetic rules of the time. Her poems contained short lines, lacked titles and often had slanted rhymes which was used to replace punctuations and capitalizations.

Although Dickinson's acquaintances knew of her writing, it was not until her death in 1886 that Dickinson's younger sister discovered her poems. It was then that her works became known to the public without any alteration by scholar Thomas H. Johnson who published *The Poems of Emily Dickinson* in 1955.

Bill Gates

He is an American business magnate born on the 28th day of October, 1955, Seattle, Washington. He grew up in an upper middle-class family with two sisters: Kristianne, the eldest and Libby, the youngest.

Bill Gates had a close relationship with his mother, Mary. She devoted her time to raise the children and worked on civil affairs and with charities. While at Lakeside School, a Seattle computer company offered to provide computer time for the students. Bill Gates spent much time with the teletype terminal for students to use and wrote a tic-tac-toe program in BASIC (a popular programming language for use on microcomputers) computer language that allowed users to play against the computer.

Bill Gates faced many challenges. One of them being a financial problem which arose when people all over the world stopped buying from him when they got to know of his age. His parents were not happy when he wanted to drop out of school to start his own company.

Bill Gates and Paul Allen founded Micro-Soft (Micro-computers and Software) in 1975 but the hyphen was dropped within a year.

As a school student, he used to brag that he would be a millionaire by the time he was 30. In reality, he became a millionaire at age 31. Had Microsoft failed to work out, he would have been an artificial intelligence researcher. His kids would only inherit a fraction of his immense wealth and his regret has been in not studying foreign languages.

Jim Carey

Actor and comedian James Eugene Carrey was born on January 17, 1962, in Newmarket, Ontario, Canada. This entertainer was unable to complete school and forced to fend for his family. Jim's form of practice was at home as he would try to cheer his mother up in the time of economic calamity. At home, Jim would make faces and rehearse in front of the mirror in his room. He had to work around his learning disability, dyslexia, in order to succeed at school. Jim's family lived in a rough district with lots of low-rent town houses. He had a rough start in life as he described himself as quiet and having no friends. One of his teachers wrote on his report card: "Jim finishes his work first and then disrupts the class." Things were not all smooth as he had to go through an eight-hour night shift with school during the day. He would be exhausted while lessons went on and feared that his school mates would discover the embarrassing poverty. He quit school at age 16. Jim quit the factory job and performed the opening act for successful comics Buddy Hackett and Rodney Dangerfield. In 1983, Carrey headed west to Hollywood where he starred in a made-for-television which led to a regular role on the hit comedy in Living Colour.

Jim Carey was rejected as a performer for the first few times such as the 1980 – '81 season of the show. With persistent efforts, he performed splendidly in films like 'Ace Ventura: Pet Detective', 'The Mask', 'Dumb and Dumber', 'Liar Liar' and 'Me, Myself and Irene.' Gradually, he began acting in more serious movies, receiving prestigious honours for his acts in films as 'The Truman Show', 'Man of the Moon' and 'How the Grinch Stole Christmas'.

In the last decade, this celebrated star was included in the 'Canadian Walk of Fame' for his cinematic achievements.

A Look into some First Borns' of their families

Oprah Winfrey [2]

On the 29th of January, 1954, Oprah Gail Winfrey was born in Kosciusko Mississippi. She grew up on a small farm, spending her earliest years with her grand mum. She moved in at the age of six with her single mother who was poor. Oprah wrote to her teacher explaining why she deserves to be moved up from kindergarten to first grade. She, Oprah, was moved up upon her teacher hearing from her with amazement at a girl her age. At the 3rd grade of school, she began to read poetry at clubs and churches. She soon became known as a "Little Speaker". She attended University at the age of 19 and took a job as a news broadcast, being an anchorwoman. She was the youngest person in Nashville to anchor a real news, then later, she started her career in the media industry. She began developing her interest when she started the early morning talk show, named, "People are talking". After moving to Chicago in 1984 to host AM Chicago, her career kicked start as a morning talk show. It became the number one talk show which she named after herself, named The Oprah Winfrey Show. Her show became the number one which was best and ranked the highest in the TV talk show in history. Oprah's talk show is watched by over 20 million people today. She is one of the richest women in the world and inspires people everywhere with her way of overcoming difficulties to be successful.

Some facts about Oprah

- She graduated high school in 1971 as the most popular student from East Nashville High School.
- She gave birth at the age of 14 to a baby boy who unfortunately died two weeks later due to complications from being born two months premature.
- Oprah holds a degree in Speech and Performing Arts for Tennessee State University

Albert Einstein

Albert Einstein was rejected in his lifetime. He wasn't considered as one who could do well in life. He had speech challenges, though his youth was marked by deep inquisitiveness and inquiry.

His parents were concerned as he was a school drop and a *draft dodger*.

On April 17, 1955 while working on a speech to honour Israel's seventh anniversary, he suffered an abnormal aortic aneurysm (a balloon-like bulge in the aorta. The large aorta that carries blood from the heart through the chest and torso. The force of blood pumping can split the layers of the artery wall, allowing blood to leak in between them.)

He was taken to a medical centre but refused surgery, believing he had lived his life and would accept his fate. He stated "I want to go when I want. It is tasteless to prolong life artificially. I have done my share, it is time to go. I will do it elegantly. He died the next morning and his brain kept for preservation.

Colonel Sanders

He was the eldest of three children to Wilbur David and Margaret Ann. Wilbur owned an 80-acre farm on which he worked until he broke his leg and then became a butcher.

Sanders became a Cook, a Farmer, Streetcar conductor, Soldier, Railroad fireman, Lawyer, Insurance salesman, Steam boat operator, Secretary, Lighting Manufacturer, Hotel Owner, Restaurateur and many more.

At age 5, his father died.

At age 16, Sanders quits school.

At age 17, he had lost four (4) jobs

At age 18, he got married. He joined the army and was driven out.

At age 20, his wife left home along with their baby.

At age 65, he retired. On the 1st day of retirement, he received a cheque from the Government for $105 which made him feel he was not able to provide for himself.

He felt like a failure and decided to commit suicide.

He borrowed $87, fried up some chicken using his recipe, went door to door to sell.

At age 88, Colonel Sanders (founder of Kentucky Fried Chicken) Empire was built.[18]

Kentucky Fried Chicken went public in 1966 and was listed on the Stock Exchange in 1969. Heublein Inc. acquired KFC Corporation in 1971 for $285 million. The brand later grew into an approximately $840 million.

Sanders continued to visit the KFC restaurants around the world as a spokesman in his later years and died at the age of 90.

J.K. ROWLING

Joanne Kathleen Rowling, an author, professionally known as J.K. Rowling. Her series of novels were published over the years 1997 -2007 and have enjoyed a great deal of commercial success. The first film in the series premiered in 2001, moved her from the status as 'an ordinary person' to a 'famous' person.

At University, J.K. Rowling studied French and the Classics. Her first husband was Portuguese but the marriage unfortunately was unsuccessful which made her cry a lot.

She was unemployed and poor.

J.K. Rowling prepared the first Harry Potter book in the Nicolson's Café in Edinburgh. Then J.K tried to find publishers in England of which she was unsuccessful with twelve (12) Publishers in England but finally found one in a scenario where a young girl happened to read the first chapter of the book and had the dad publishing it.

Six more books have been written and films also.

The world's wealthiest people did not have it all in their families, they started from somewhere and they are where they are not by chance and time only but a choice to be better persons.

The first of all things (human, animals, plants, fruits) signifies the beginning of beautiful things. It is a sign of productivity as it creates the path for the others to pass through. As a farmer, I walked through my field and noticed the seeds in the soil germinate as tiny as special weeds growing from the earth. I smiled as to the sign of fruitfulness in the field and the produce from the harvest to come. When seedlings are grown in desert areas or stony fields and does not yield usually after a period of time, it is noted as an area where a particular specie is not likely to survive if any other of the same kind were to be planted there. A different ground frame would be used to test for later seedlings as to whether it would thrive or not, why? Because the first seedlings did not make it so it becomes research. In rare cases, it takes longer for certain species to germinate in a particular field in which no other seedling would be grown during the time of unproductivity from the soil above. The question again, why? A second seedling being grown in a land where the first did not work is more likely, the second would not grow.

Companies as Apple would cherish the first group of workers it had because they made a mark. Had they failed in their belief to build something out of nothing, later generations would not have come to meet the products which the world appreciates now. The first group of people Jesus Christ chose to spread the good news of God's Kingdom died as Matyrs and are remembered till now. The first believers of a particular religion (Christianity) did it and the gospel became famous even in their death, their words lived in the hearts of those who heard it. Had the first disciples failed in their quest to spread the Gospel and not died as Matyrs, other generations would not have followed their paths.

Why is the first born not noticed?

Forgetfulness is a sign of taking everything as a normal routine and not as reference to learn and build on what has been achieved or done. Many a time, a country that forgets its history, a company that ignores the effort of the first crop of people it had or a particular individual making a difference, usually do not do well after some time. Companies that have been handed over to sons and daughters to take over from the Visionaire or Founder, comes to an end mostly. Most often inherited children take it for granted that tiresome nights and hardwork has gone into a brand. At other times, their interest from the start may be different from that of the parents.

The first son normally carries the burden of catering for the younger siblings, an in-born trait which most carry all through their life. A responsibility that lies unforeseen to the younger ones. Events in life could make younger ones prosper than the first, grow as someone the family looks up to but the first son in his success or failure still carries a mark of a leader when ushered into an unknown family. Every individual has the destiny and one becomes who he or she wants to be by will (choice) or association (friends). We are 'First Borns' if positive change is to occur in a family or nation. We are 'First Borns' if the sense of Responsibility to make lives better, lies in us. No one is born by accident, though it may seem so if born out of chance and orphaned in an abandoned world. The book called *The Child Called It* tells of a child who was abandoned, fed from the streets but had his end not in shame. A decision to make life better lies from within us as a 'First Born'. The sperm that survived over a million sperms.

The First Born lives in us all, The First Born to make generations to come to be proud of us, The First Born that never dies until we consciously want it to die.

The assurance

There is an assurance that no matter one's place of birth or the number of siblings before you, you can make it in this life. There are instances where people were neither first kids from their parents but have set the pace for others to have confidence that they also can make it in life.

Mankind has been designed differently and exceptional. There is a world of possibilities and greater height to be achieved. The only limitation is our self. Challenges are a part of life activities; it makes one stronger when we face them by perseverance. Dreams, visions, goals, do not just happen, it takes work. Practical steps are involved; having the imagination is good but not enough to carry you to the level or height to be attained.

Biblical verses to encourage all persons

When you pass through the waters, I will be with you; and through the rivers, they shall not overwhelm you; when you walk through fire you shall not be burned, and the flame shall not consume you – Isaiah 43:2.

From a similar verse in the Bible, Isaiah 41: 10 says that "fear not, for I am with you; be not dismayed, for I am your God; I will strengthen you, I will help you, I will uphold you with my righteous hand – Isaiah 41:10.

So we can confidently say, "The Lord is my helper; I will not fear; what can man do to me?" – Hebrews 13: 6-7

In the beginning, God created the heaven and the earth. Why an inhabitation in the first place? Some place to lay the head and call home. When it seems difficult, there your result is closest.

Joseph (Biblical Character)

Genesis 36 – 50 talks of the birth and death of a man who made a difference in his time. At the age of 17, Joseph fed the flock with his brothers. He was loved by his dad because he was his son of his old age: and he made a coat of many colours for him. Joseph was a dreamer who loved to narrate his dreams to his brothers and sister named Dinah. The more he narrated his dreams to his brothers, the more they hated him. He was sold to Egypt for slavery. He had to serve a Master named Potiphar. Joseph eventually used this dream to save Egypt from famine. He becomes a leader in charge of food in the country, brings his siblings together and stands out as a 'first born'. He did not have it easy as a slave, serving his Master, going to prison and eventually coming out as a leader with influence in Egypt.

Joseph even finally becomes the first born, though he was the last but one child of his father.

The firstborn of Israel (Reuben) lost his position because he defiled his father's couch; he lost his birthright, so that he could not be enrolled as the oldest son".

Abel (Biblical Character)

In the Bible, from Genesis 4, there is the story of two siblings where each of them decides to go on a project which has different outcomes. The older son has his project, not satisfactory whilst the younger one has his offering accepted. Anger, pain, hatred and all evil thoughts, sets in the heart of Cain. Cain kills his brother, Abel, who has his accepted and denies knowing his whereabouts.

Though Abel was the second son, let us learn from his actions as a 'FIRST BORN'. Abel brought the firstborn of his flock and of their fat portions. And the Lord had regard for Abel and his offering.

We need one another to encourage, strengthen, assure ourselves that giving up is not the only way but facing the challenges life offers, makes us achievers.

CHAPTER TWO

Knowledge

GOOD BOY / BAD BOY SYNDROME

In the Ghanaian culture mainly, children are trained to be respectful to the older generation, always greeting and being obedient.

These are good morals that shape the child to a bright future. In the Bible, the book of Proverbs says: "Train up a child and when he grows, he will not depart from it".

What do we understand by good boy or bad boy?

'Good boy' normally refers to a child who is quiet, isolated and not poking in people's businesses.

On the other hand, 'bad boy' refers to a rude, curious, problematic and 'out-of-the-norm' person.

Many of Mankind are in the 'Good boy' category in the sense that we are much comfortable in the states we find ourselves in. In most cases, it's something we need assistance or miracles to get to the dream. This dream never happens because it takes pain, sacrifice, commitment and trying over and over without letting go or giving up. If it were easy to get to the heights we all desire, then everyone would be successful. Surprisingly, some grew up very poor but beat the odds because of the desire to perfect the little skill they had and dedicated much time to it.

The very few who stand out are the people who move out of the norm.

A brief look into the world of Inventors' (Bad Boy).

This is a look into the world of people considered to behave in ways which does not conform to society's standard.

The man who invented the light (Thomas Edison)

This is a story of a child rising from rags to riches. There is a famous quote of him saying, "Genius is one percent inspiration and ninety-nine percent perspiration." He would work for 72 hours stretch in order to perfect an invention. He believed there were no such things as mistakes as long as you learned from them. He was known to be a great prankster. He would treat his employees with sing along, poetry contests and satirical writings. It is a blend of hobby in work which makes every mistake as a pattern of knowledge added to the ideas gathered. Young Edison, was kicked out of school for asking too many questions. A quote of this young man says "If I find 10,000 ways something wouldn't work, I haven't failed".

These people went out of their way (bad-boy's) to do such beautiful things.

Surprisingly, the first person to think and study into airplanes is not the Wright brothers but a man named Samuel Langley. Many of us don't know him because he was discouraged many times and called it 'quit'. Not all that glitters, is gold is a common quote in our time. Nothing beautiful comes easy. If he (Samuel Langley) had succeeded, he would have been praised as a 'good child' and probably celebrated with him. But now who knows him…

An insight into Samuel Langley's Life

Samuel was a guy who devoted much time to solar physics which made him achieve a unit for measuring solar radiation, named the Langley. He received honorary degrees but still felt unfulfilled and intellectually isolated from mainstream science. Israel Lancaster presented a paper with many theoretical errors that the assembly of professionals felt ashamed because of the reports by the newspaper agencies. This presented Samuel with a new challenge. In 1891, Langley wrote a paper that mechanical flight was possible with engines. Lightness, strength and power were necessities for planes or Aerodromes as he called it. In 1901, Samuel built a quarter-size model that flew successfully. Aerodromes were built and tested several times with different applications, designs and engines. At almost 62 years, Langley hires Edward Chalmers Huffaker to assist him. Edward was not however the only person Samuel had hired to assist in the contribution of the Aerodromes. Aerodrome No. 5 flew to a maximum altitude of 80 feet with estimated calculations at 90 seconds between 20 and 25 mph, travelling about 3,300 feet. This was the first in aerial navigation as the astounded members applauded the effort with shouts and cheers including observers who witnessed the event. Alexander Graham Bell, a friend and a fellow scientist to Samuel made this quote "It seems to me that no one who was present on this interesting occasion could have failed to recognize that the practicality of mechanical flight had been demonstrated".

Ice-breaker on Samuel's life and history

On December 8, 1903, Aerodrome No. 5 powered by gasoline engine had similar problems to early steam-powered models. With money being exhausted and heavy public want for results, Samuel abandons his desire for powered, manned, heavier than air flight project. Ironically, 9 days after that decision, the world's successful flight of that kind was performed by Wilbur and Orville Wright. The Wright brothers have it in records now that they were the first to fly. That last moment decision by Samuel of not heeding to the cries of the public, though he flew the first aircraft above the ground for some minutes, had his name wiped out of the mouths of many generations.

A feeling of being a Bad Boy

In the Bible, John 3:1-21 speaks of Nicodemus who came to Jesus by NIGHT and said unto Him, Rabbi we (Pharisee's) know that thou art a teacher. Nicodemus was a ruler of the Jews. I am sure he didn't go there to ask about 'born again' topics there but to know how much Jesus knows and His secrets. Being a bad boy means asking lots of questions, finding out why things are in a particular way or the reason behind an idea.

Nicodemus is seen as a 'good' person, a well-respected individual in society and an Elder who would not want to soil his image by visiting Jesus in the day. Nicodemus had to find a way to see Jesus at night. He could not have done this without sneaking and disguising himself.

It is a good feeling when the step in getting a deeper understanding on a topic is known. The real meaning to a situation when the general view has been misleading for a long time is achieved when inquisitive. Nicodemus would have felt great in understanding why rumours went in a direction to the real happening.

The architect and constructor of the first boat (Noah – A Biblical Character)

Here comes a time when wickedness is everywhere. The Lord tells this man to build a boat to prepare humans and animals in one place. Lots of hours went into the building of this boat when none had been made and no rain had fallen. On the last day of finishing, lots of people saw the picture he had in mind to reality. It took consistency and years in working at it.

The uniqueness

The Good and Bad boy have their differences unique in their own way.

The Good and Bad boy lies in us all, it is in our nature to explore, ask questions and make mistakes.

The Good and Bad boy should not be classified and treated differently, we all need to be refined to make us better persons.

THE UNCONSCIOUS DEATH

The things we see and hear everyday shapes our ability to work on particular things and to behave according to information. Thousands of messages come to us each day, some may be true and others false. The Bible says from Romans 10:17 that Faith comes by hearing and hearing by the Word of God. Each time we feed ourselves with good information, the more renewed Man becomes in strength and knowledge.

I tune in to my favourite radio station as I start the vehicle. As I reach the workplace, I am surrounded by the wonderful works of nature; the plants, birds, trees and the freshness of the air that welcomes me. This I enjoy when I arrive and close from the workplace. My mind is made up of the news I watch at night and the radio I listen to in the morning. My fellow colleagues argue on issues and society directs my life with the several waves of information surrounding me.

One Saturday, I happened to surf the internet to get myself abreast with the events trending. Pages and icons of different types from different websites popped up. To my amazement on clicking on a subject which read 'Poisonous plants you never knew about'. It got me interested to read more, I had seen pictures of the plants on the internet at my workplace which I recognized with ease. In fact, I had some at home from a neighbour which I used to nicely decorate the borders of my house. This plant is called the "Dumb Cane" or Dieffenbachia. It was a plant used to punish slaves and by having some leaves in the mouth, could cause one to have throat paralysis and result in loss of voice (HubPages,2009).

There is a chemical stronger than DDT which is being used for fertilizing food crops. One particular type of such strong fertilizers is coated around the maize seedlings and planted in the soil. The effects of this particular fertilizer leaves the bees very weak in their combs, unable to move and shaking as the effect of the fertilizer gets into them by the air carrying such molecules from the fertilizer. Now it is being produced in large quantities and humans consume these maize products while the bees are even rendered unproductive in their normal duties. In my part of the world, there are good soils rich in soil nutrients to produce food but at the mention of 'Made in....' from an European Nation, there is no doubt about the quality of the product being purchased. Neonicotinoids is a type of insecticide which causes a bee colony to collapse. Bees make honey and if these insecticides render them unproductive, same would happen to Man over a long period of time.

There is a regular advert on the radio stations in my locality and beyond on the news about the sweet fragrance of a mosquito spray. Insecticides are meant to kill insects, so the more humans inhale it, over a long period of time, it gets into their bodies and would eventually cause damage to the internal organs. This damage is evident but would not be disclosed as harmful on the advert as its sales would be affected when the harm is also made known of. Fragrance is meant to change the atmosphere, making it pleasant to enjoy, not to inhale as an insecticide.

The scratch card on which credits are loaded onto my phone has to be peeled off and is mostly done by using the finger nail. In a haste to load the credits on it, the debris is blown off and the remaining particles in the nail is left forgotten. The finger is used to eat snacks, petty food and shake hands without necessarily washing the hands with water and soap. What I do not know is the danger of using my hands to eat snacks with particles from the scratch card, thereby carrying germs to the body.

There was a newly paved out route which obviously had no traffic light, all four routes have to pass through a channel for their exits. Honking cars all over with some trying to take shorter channels to their various destinations, caused problems to all. Everybody wants to move at the same time and the drivers from behind would honk at those who had the opportunity to go through, to hasten so they can eventually pass through. In a certain European country, drivers move in fours (4's). The first four cars move while the others wait, the next four move, with all other vehicles waiting for their turn. This cycle continues and there is smooth transition without the help of a traffic warden. This pattern moved quicker than the one I observed in my locality where everyone wanted a bite of the cake.

Getting rich and dying younger is a thing that most adverts and movies insinuate. Drinking alcohol for sexual strengths and its lasting effect on the human body is said to be the power of a man. A man is showcased with a beautiful lady by his side, with the drink on one side of the hand while the deception lies mostly on the youth to express themselves by having the strength to dominate their female counterparts.

I die also from the inability to think on my own, to create and provide solutions to the environment. Things I hear and see control my circle of life and I die unconsciously from friends, my surrounding and from the media mostly. Calculators were tools used for complex tasks by professionals but the 'Mental' drill was more efficient. As far as I could remember, the multiplication table was one thing that made one think faster.

One question that has gone missing is 'how the people of old lived longer?' Now, the current generation seem to have a shorter life span. Could it be from alcohol, drugs from the pharmacy, the food we eat, pressure to get rich quickly or dying while trying? What could have gone wrong? In our fast pace world, I can only think that our generation falls into the systems of life, having no knowledge of life's challenges and dying unconsciously.

The slow death is a pain that occurs in a person especially in situations where no answers can be found. Verbal abuse and depression is a few of the many things that kill persons from within. In the part of the world I come from, who do you report to? Everyone has issues and it is up to individuals to figure out the answer for themselves. Will a friend spread my worries to fellow colleagues or be used against me some time?

The Unconscious Death lies in words spoken without taking time to digest the words. It lies in information one hears and in the system where high blood pressure builds from within because no one is interested in another man's issues.

The meditation of the Scriptures in the Bible and fellowshipping with one's Maker is ideal. Humans can hardly be trusted but a few ones that can,are avenues to release 'missiles' from within should be encouraged and not seen as a weakness. The male especially is brought up not to share his problems as it is seen as a 'weakness' - even with a respectable leader (Counsellor).

Man has problems and it is part of our existence - no one can avoid. It is in speaking out our heart to the few ones one trusts, that makes us better. Communication to our Maker such as in the case of David the King and Moses (both in the Old Testament) spoke to God in prayer.

David and Jonathan also had a strong friendship in a positive way.

Good information and neglect of bad information which comes to Man has to be analysed before it affects one either positively or negatively.

Lots of information would come to us, what matters is to read a lot, know the truth behind a matter and acquire information. Not all things are true, not all are false either.

Isaiah 5:13 – 14

Therefore my people go into exile **for lack of knowledge**; their honoured men go hungry, and their multitude is parched with thirst. Therefore, Sheol has enlarged its appetite and opened its mouth beyond measure, and the nobility of Jerusalem and her multitude will go down, her merrymakers and he who exults in her.

I AM PRESIDENT

I am an architect; I design buildings depending on the needs of my clients. My fellow colleagues do design but with no advise to their clients as to what is involved or what should be added and subtracted from the draft. I do free counsel sessions with my customers and I do it well. I am being recommended by many because it is professional and I am welcoming. I am envied by my fellow architects as in bringing smiles on people's faces and also not charging them excessively. This is my office, I am President.

I am a driver who transports farm produce to the market. It's a new adventure I am into but from the words of my fellow drivers, there is more to know and learn from. The roads are bad from the villages we get the vegetables, fruits and food items from, so the drivers drive fast on the roads knowing very well the tyres and other parts of the car will be faulty but they would move for money. The more items you send, the more you earn. At the end of the day, the damaged cars are returned to their respective owners for repairs. I take my time to drive and create good relationships between the farmers from the village and the traders. I maintain a high standard; I have had success in terms of saving money on the car breakdown and time at the mechanics. The value placed on me cannot be replaced by how high I raise the price of goods, tell a lie or damage my Superior's vehicle. As it is known in my country, a soldier is more respected in his uniform than the policeman. This is not written in books or said openly, but in the minds of 'us' the citizens.

This is my office I am President.

I am a painter; I give designs to the interior and exterior parts of the home or office. I make it attractive and relaxing for my customers to feel at home. I go out of the ordinary and add value to my work. The colours that match up with the brush of lines on the wall is a marvel to many. From the simplest form of ideas to the most complex form of tasks, I do it with my heart and passion.

This is my office, I am President.

CHAPTER THREE

The Realities of Life

IN AND AFTER CHURCH

I glanced through the crowd to notice the expression on the faces of individuals as the theme for the Sunday's topic 'Importance of the Cross' was being preached. Before me and behind, I noticed most people dosing off, heads bowed down with some carrying dark spectacles to shade off the sleep.

A friend's grand mum told me of angels who stand at the entrance of the Church to bless those walking in and out after church service. Testimonies of people witnessing angels blessing individuals during church who have receptive hearts and forgiving spirits. So many a time, the devil distracts the attention of the Congregation with the cry of babies, unnecessary conversation by a neighbouring Christian or a thought of an event. Not all of these noises are necessarily from the adversary, some occur from our human willingness not to listen. Falling down during anointing services does not necessarily mean the work of the Holy Spirit, it is not scriptural to fall or not but it is necessary to test all spirits and know the Lord for yourself. Thus, after preaching this Word for the day lots of people could remember the praises and adoration as the apex of the church service. Many congregants had virtually forgotten about the lessons of the Word preached.

A young Pastor spoke to a group of people after church service, the atmosphere remained calm and hunger to receive whatever would come out from the mouth of the Pastor. After a few minutes of reading from the older Pastor's book to the congregation, people began falling without laying on of hands. Some gave testimonies of what had happened in the course of the previous week to the members around.

This young Pastor met this particular group after church always and the testimonies and joyful cries would be poured out each week with fresh anointing. The secret of this small sect of people receiving blessings after church to my observation was not of the age of the young Pastor. They believed God first, had no hurt or envy for anyone and they were eager to be fed as sheep from the Shepherd.

Others were so in tune as to write the messages on paper. Some shamefaced, recalling their actions in their minds and judging their deeds to these plain words of salvation. And in the silence, I wondered how the heart of the hearers throb; as if heaven's anger had dawned on us. Yet all the energies filled the people after the last grace was shared. All the soberness had disappeared; the original intents of the masses becoming clearer. It was a norm, a tradition without real surface. What is the point of all this if our lives are not transformed after church? Age doesn't matter before God, intimacy with him makes the difference. Every other blessing is a bonus gift IN AND AFTER CHURCH – Ebo Awotwe

> After church, attitudes of individuals tend to remain the same. Why does it happen after each Sunday?
> Matthew 13:18- 23

"Hear then the parable of the sower: When anyone hears the word of the kingdom and does not understand it, the evil one comes and snatches away what has been sown in his heart. This is what was sown on rocky ground, this is the one who hears the word and immediately receives it with joy, yet he has no root in himself, but endures for a while, and when tribulation or persecution arises on account of the word, immediately he falls away. As for what was sown among thorns, this is the one who hears the word, but the cares of the world and the deceitfulness of riches choke the word, and it proves unfaithful. As for what was sown on good soil, this is the one who hears the word and understands it. He indeed bears fruit and yields in one case a hundredfold, in another sixty, and in another thirty."

The few that do change after church is a reflection of the Message being preached and 'Grace' that makes us have a change of heart and mind, like Paul who wrote most of the letters in the New Testament.

A Daily Walk and Meditation on the Word of God makes us New in our lives IN AND AFTER CHURCH.

BEHIND THE SHADE

The complication of the human system makes it an interesting one as no one can predict the outcome of a person unless the end of an individual is almost too visible to avoid. Some have adapted a strategy to survive in this adverse time Man finds him or herself in. It is only a Man that can smile with the animal it wants to kill.

As innocent as one walks on the earth, there are plans by other persons on how well the new job went, the marriage, the new car, the first child of the family, change of position at the work place and many more. There are people watching each time an action is carried out by an individual, whether consciously or unconsciously.

It is said that the bird has learnt to fly without perching and so has the hunter learnt to shoot without missing. An individual in society is more respected especially when he or she is financially stable and influential. As a kid growing up around the blocks in the vicinity, there were things I heard and wondered why and what happened to make an event occur? An event such as false accusation in the court room which leads to an arrest of an innocent person for years languishing in jail. What could have been the influence of such a witness? It is surprising watching these events as a movie and the toil it takes the hero to come out of the situation. Does this case happen each time an innocent person finds himself coming out blamelessly? No.

The Human mind cannot be easily told what is going on for it is simple and complex. While smiling and laughing, there is another motive behind the smile. Some cry in their celebration and others in afflictions. Some jubilate when the desired results are achieved whether good or bad. The world is a system in which Man gets into it and plays by the rules. A journalist for instance would interview a person and depending on how well the cards are laid on the table, would tell whether one is exposing himself or not. An interview would begin with congratulations on particular projects, achievements, how the achievements came into existence and why certain particular issues occur within the same sector where an individual boast of his or her achievements. By this time, instead of a straight forward question which was to be asked, a merry-go-round tale would have existed playing on the mind. There is nothing to fear when an individual is clean and without fault to be truthful.

Truth is an expensive commodity in our time as Man covers his image with pretense. Some hide behind the efforts of skilled workers to get things done as a team, others to claim wealth by engaging in illegal works at night. The night is so dark in the human mind that it exists any time of the day. In a busy market square where individuals engage in trading, others have their 'night' times in operation. A property that belonged to you before entering the market area goes missing when one gets to a destination when it is finally noticed that it is gone. Who made Man survive by taking from a person what he or she has not sweated for? Is it the system of the family, environment or the country? I dream of a place where food items are placed in a table and buyers come for them leaving the money under the food item and leaving without the seller being present and none stealing from it. I would want to experience such a feeling of going home with the exact amount of money under the tray to prevent the winds from blowing it away. The system of the world wants to move into a cashless system because of trust. A thumb print or strong password is placed on the card to make it difficult for others to steal even when they have accessed the card. Yes, it may be done but it is the same human mind which can place a 'DENY' on a card through administrative functions to deny a particular person or to withdraw money by hacking into the card. The night activities exist in the system where power is the home of happiness. I see a man toil all day and taxed for the little earned and the rich taking from the tax. It is a good thing when taxes are used for the right purpose but is it the case where accountability is asked of persons when functions do not get started as scheduled and the money smoked into the air? Positions for organisations from school right up the ladder to Presidency has manipulations as to who the favourite is to win a spot in contesting for a leadership role which is done though people who are influential.

An anxious moment awaits us all in our various fields of endeavor as to who stays in the game of survival. Meetings and counter-arguments are held over the few of us who have to stay to manage the industry. After several nervous moments, the time comes finally to know who qualifies to stay and leave. The results are mentioned and it all occurred in a room far from our hearing and so is life. To be in a place at a particular time sometimes requires decisions you as a person has to take or someone in a chamber is having with another person on recommending or suggesting otherwise as to a place one has to be in. In a particular workshop I was privileged to attend, it was based on recommendation.

There was a woman with the issue of blood in the Bible who could not go out for years. She then heard of Jesus' name being mentioned. Then she decided to come out and touch a hem of The Masters' Garment to be healed. It was a decision taken which changed her situation and life even to the attention of virtue leaving the Master.

Another lady called Mary Magdalene made a decision to bless the Lord Jesus with an expensive oil. Faith was mixed with works and with that level of sacrifice, it attracted a blessing for her. Her name has been mentioned in the Bible and her name known through generations. That was a time when women were not regarded in the gathering of men or worthy to fight for their country.

Behind every shade is a tear, envy, strife, hatred, love and many more. Both the good and bad exists behind the shade. Choose the right things in the 'night' to reflect in the 'day'.

To have things turned around for ones sake, there are decisions we as human need to take personally, work on them and talk to our Creator for blessings on the works of our hands.

The 'night' is our shade.

What is behind your shade?

CHRISTIAN ON SUNDAY
SINNER ON MONDAY

My journey begins from society, experience in life (near death experiences, miracles from close relations, happy-sad moments with people, what I hear and how true information is) and my assessment of events in life.

One Saturday evening I made up my mind to visit a particular church I had heard much stories of. On Sunday mornings, the streets are full of gospel songs, songs playing on air, songs emanating from the windows of rooms, such a ceremony embraced by all like a religious festivity on time bomb. Every *nook and cranny* in the rooms of homes and radio stations was filled with sweet melodies.

Our Saviour Jesus Christ said greater things shall we do than He did. Peter, the disciple of Jesus Christ, had his shadow healing a sick person. The Apostle Paul who did not meet Jesus Christ wrote most of the letters in the New Testament and said *He considers what he has done as anything but he is focused on what lies ahead.* Light shines in the dark and darkness comprehends not *John 1:4.* No matter where believers of Christ find themselves, they should be noticed as the transformer. Why hide when *a city on a hill cannot be hidden but is seen by all?* No matter how hard we (Christians) would want to be invisible, not noticed, our words and deeds should still be light. *If you are shy to preach my Word, I would be shy to talk of you to my Father who is in Heaven.* The Lord sees the heart of all who diligently seek Him, not those who lift hands and cry in public places to be noticed.

Behaviour should not be changed on particular days or times or seasons due to circumstances unless changed for the better which should last. Chameleons are adaptive creatures in the sense that their colours change according to the environment to prevent them from being noticed by their prey. This strategy rather is to be used to convert others to believe in the Lord who had to come down in the form of Man to deliver His people from sin. The Father loved us so much that He gave His only begotten son to die for Man-kind. Love your neighbour as yourself, He who gives his riches and dies for another but has no love, cannot make it to the Kingdom of God. God is love and he who says he has no love is not of God. Christians ought to love.

It is one thing to be born a Christian and another to be a Christian. There is another thing to profess Christ and another thing to have a personal relationship with Him. It is good to praise and worship the Lord but better if the praise and worship is from the heart and not from the lips. Christians are to be the salt, for if the salt loses its flavour it shall be trampled upon.

Paul I know, Titus I know, but who are you? (Romans 13:1-7). The Lord knows His people *(John 10:5)*.

I wished that thou art either cold or hot but not both (Rev 3:15). It is better to be who you are and allow the Lord help in times of weaknesses and strengths. A Christian trying to please particular persons makes the change in us not worth following. Our lights as we live and walk and talk is to be a reflection of the Saviour we follow.

Be a Christian every day and Sinners will be converted by the Words and Actions we (Christian's) portray.

WEAK WEEK

I wake up in the morning in search of the recent and upcoming messages on my social media. I stretch and jump out of bed to do my chores. My day has already been planned by an organizer inserted in my memory. The hustle and bustle of the day sends my restless body to bed after a day's schedule of activities.

My off-days from work are the time I have for the numerous movie series and the 'outings' with friends especially on holidays. Do I have time for my Christian walk with my Maker? Yes, I go to church on Sundays from 7am – 9am where I read the bible, sing hymns and see my church friends. Probably, after long periods of absenteeism, I would show my face off to the church folks that I am present. After a year of my job, I begin feeling weak spiritually. There is no connection between myself and my Maker in terms of prayer and His Word (Bible).

A leave is not something I enjoy particularly, I would rather sell it but this time I am in front of the doctor. A young beautiful fair lady with a pair of glasses on and a wide smile with the teeth sparkling as the rise of the early morning sun. She has a ring on the finger I notice, but who cares if she is married. Cheating is no wrong if I am the 'King of Chess'. The right moves ought to be done and '*voila*', the fish would be caught in the net, 'Checkmate'.

I asked the young doctor out and exchanged contacts. Persistence draws the doctor close to me and far from her home with the ticking of the clock and the days coming and leaving.

The body is a framework of systems which needs to be maintained like an engine. My body system broke down and I reminisced how nice it was to be healthy. I had not exercised and thus become obese. A sexually transmitted disease I was told to have contracted from the sexual lifestyle I had engaged in got me thinking deeply into life's matters. My life is in shambles now. This week of illness got me thinking of the right things I stopped doing.

The right thing is to wake up in the morning, say a prayer of thanksgiving and read the bible. If time be, some few push-ups and skipping would do.

The doctor had taken my contact after a hard laugh at a joke I cracked. She visits me often and tells me to get well quickly. We shared wonderful moments and the adventures of the 'world' to be explored.

My Bible is a tool to carry for church services, leaving the reading to the Pastor as it is his job requirement to preach. Well-known men and women got invited to the front for donations, fund-raising, appeals, church projects and so on, none cared how each one of us became rich, all that mattered was to give and receive the praises of the leaders. That at least gave me opportunities and reasons to go to church. I became strong two weeks after the hospital visit and frequently met the doctor in a nearby café for few shots of alcohol. Our relationship became intimate, we spent lesser times with our individual spouses, had sex and enjoyed going out especially, spending nights at the motel which had in-built swimming pools for the crème-de la-crème in the society. Life is short they say, enjoy whiles it lasts.

A decade passes by with our individual families and society praising my lovely doctor and me at separate places for contributing our quota to society. Our relationship was out of public notice and from marital homes.

What goes into the body, at a point would show by how good or bad it's been treated from the start. Both the doctor and myself contracted no viruses, but there was something worrying somewhere. My businesses begun failing, my kids were falling ill on regular basis whiles the doctor also lost her license to practise after a weird incidence at the workplace over the death of a patient under her watch. Spiritual things I know are for the fetish and the prophets but these events rang bells to my ears that I need to go for spiritual help.

My finances were racing down the lane to 'bankruptcy'. As two months passed by I was in the news for abusing a graduate seeking job at my firm with a video footage of me taking advantage of her predicament. Everything was going down the drain. Shortly after, charges were being pressed against me, my health would deteriorate with the knowledge of a low blood pressure which is most dangerous according to medical facts.

Days and weeks passed by while things got worse. A business associate advised I visit a pastor from his church to pray for me as it seemed was the solution to my plight. We got to the church and upon seeing me, the Pastor said I should ask for forgiveness from my wife and kids for the extra-marital affairs I had had. I clenched my fists and ground my teeth to show my enraged fury at this young hungry-looking man who had asked me to ask for forgiveness from my family. The situation was too much to contain. I asked my Heavenly Father to forgive me and as I did I remembered an old Sunday School rhyme which says 'Read your bible, pray everyday if you want to grow'. Nothing changed about the health and finances after a while but a load of some sort was lifted off my shoulders. Now, I don't only go to church but I am serious with my Christian life, marriage and attitude towards people.

Thanks to this young Pastor, I am a man now with love from my family again as they forgave me to make me whole again.

No more would I be weak in a week.

REFERENCES ON THE
FIRST BORN

[1] Online at https://megaslides.com/doc/5199231/birth-order-effects

[2] Available at http://www.notablebiographies.com/We-Z/Winfrey-Oprah.html [Accessed: 10/12/2016]

[3] Wikimedia Foundation, Inc, 2016, Emily Dickinson. Creative Commons Attributions-Share Alike License

[4] Roland Lazenby, 2014. Michael Jordan: The Life

[5] Greene, Bob. *Hang Time*. New York: Doubleday, 1992.

[6] Gutman, Bill. *Michael Jordan: A Biography*. New York: Pocket Books, 1991.

[7] Halberstam, David. *Playing for Keeps: Michael Jordan and the World He Made*. New York: Random House, 1999.

[8] Jordan, Michael. *For the Love of the Game: My Story*. New York: Crown Publishers, 1998.

[9] Naughton, Jim. *Taking to the Air: The Rise of Michael Jordan*. New York: Warner Books, 1992.

[10] Smith, Sam. *The Jordan Rules*. New York: Simon and Schuster, 1992.

[11] Available at related:www.notablebiographies.com/Jo-Ki/Jordan-Michael.html michael jordan challenges in his life [Accessed: 03/12/2016]

[12] Available at https://thebestten.wordpress.com/the-evolution-of-michael-jordan/ [Accessed: 03/12/2016]

[13] Available at http://mmdnge.blogspot.com/2012/08/facts-about-michael-jordan-life.html

[Accessed: 03/12/2016]

[14] Sally Terrones,2013. Michael Jordan – Overcoming An Obstacle

[15] Available at http://famous-relationships.topsynergy.com/Albert_Einstein/Challenges.asp [Accessed: 26/12/2016]

[16] Available at http://www.theverge.com/2016/7/5/12096466/colonel-sanders-kfc-meme-life-story [Accessed: 29/12/2016]

[17] Available at http://www.thefamouspeople.com/profiles/colonel-sanders-3728.php [Accessed: 29/12/2016]

[18] Available at http://www.biography.com/people/colonel-harland-sanders-12353545#kentucky-fried-chicken-is-born [Accessed: 30/12/2016]

[19] Bill Gates. (2011). *Biography.com.* Retrieved 02:17, Aug 28 2011 from http://www.biography.com/articles/Bill-Gates-9307520

[20] www.thefamouspeople.com/privacy-policy.php [Accessed: 31/12/2016]

Biblical texts were taken from the Good News Translation, King James Version and the New King James Version

www.ingramcontent.com/pod-product-compliance
Lightning Source LLC
Chambersburg PA
CBHW030527290526
45786CB00004B/1655